15 Stories to learn French For kids

French is now the fifth most
spoken world language.

Make your kids learn a new language.

French-English Stories.

Why Learning a new Language is Important?

Creativity is increased with the study of foreign languages. Foreign languages provide a competitive edge in career choices (assure a better future): one is able to communicate in a second language. Foreign language study enhances listening skills and memory.

Benefits of Learning a Second Language at an Early Age?

Research shows that learning a second language at an Early Age boosts problem-solving, critical-thinking, and listening skills, in addition to improving memory, concentration, and the ability to multitask. Children proficient in other languages also show signs of enhanced creativity and mental flexibility.

Why French?

First and foremost, learning French is the pleasure of learning a beautiful, rich, melodious language that is often called the language of love. French is also an analytical language that structures thought and develops critical thinking, which is a valuable skill for discussions and negotiations.

Summary

Salut!

STORIES WITH MORALS

Story 1: THE STELLAR ONE

When the universe was JEUNE the sky was filled with planets, and ÉTOILES, and stardust, and many many rocks.
One of these rocks was a bit more special than the rest. She was unlike any that came before her.

She was a GENTIL and HEUREUX rock, who always floated near a big BLEU planet.
Sometimes when the LUMIÈRE hit her surface, she would glow a brilliant green. At times like those, she almost didn't look like a rock at all.

As the sky moved from JOUR to JOUR, and week to week, the rock would see planets far off in the distance.
She would wonder what it would be like to go to them. Week after week and month after month she would wonder. Until one day she decided to DÉCOUVRIR.

JEUNE = Young   ÉTOILES = Stars
GENTIL = Kind   HEUREUX = Happy
BLEU = Blue   LUMIÈRE = Light
JOUR = Day   DÉCOUVRIR = Discover

The rock had never gone anywhere AVANT and
wasn't sure how to go about it.
She started to rock back and forth.
Then she started to spin.
Soon enough, she was VOLER through the sky.
As she left, DES NUAGES swirled on the big blue
planet. For it was sad to see her go, and when
planets cry there is a PLUIE storm.

At first the rock was PAS good at moving. She
would spin too LOIN to the right or too far to the
left. Slowly she learned how to travel whichever
direction she liked, and she enjoyed exploring
L'ESPACE.

She saw a planet filled AVEC water, with not a
speck of land.

Then found a planet all dried up, with beaches
made of SABLE.

AVANT = Before   VOLER = Flying
DES NUAGES = Clouds   PLUIE = Rain
PAS = Not   LOIN = Far
L'ESPACE = Space   AVEC = With
SABLE = Sand

ELLE swore she met a planet who looked
suspiciously like her.

And then she saw a planet that was, well... she
wasn't sure.

One planet she discovered, had grown forests made
of VERT.

Another one was very shy, not fond of being seen.

She flew right by a planet, that was frozen icy cold.

And then she saw a planet that was made of jewels
and gold!

She had started to notice that each PLANÈTE
seemed brighter than the DERNIÈRE.
They were all so different and all so pretty.

ELLE = She   VERT = Green
PLANÈTE = Planet   DERNIÈRE = Last

It became DURE for her to decide where to go next.
If each planet she visited was PLUS beautiful than
the one before it, then how could she decide which
way to PARTIR next, and how could she decide
where to RESTER.
So she continued traveling, afraid to miss a single
planet.
Eventually she came upon the GRANDE blue planet
that she had once circled, but she found that is was
not the same. It was shining in a way that it never
had before. It was more blue than it had ever been,
and certainly more BELLE.

This made her stop for a MOMENT.
"I do not know where I should go next" she said out
loud. "Each direction is filled with wonderful planets.
And I cannot STOP, knowing that the next planet will
be even more beautiful if I continue on. Even my big
blue planet has grown more beautiful every day in
my absence."

DURE = Hard   PLUS = More
PARTIR = Go   RESTER = Stay
GRANDE = Big   BELLE = Beautiful
MOMENT = Moment   STOP = Stop

The big blue planet overheard this. "Can you not see POURQUOI I am brighter?" it asked.

"You are the brightest planet I have ever VU," she said, "but I do not know why you glow brighter today than you did when I left you."

"You have brightened MOI," it said.

"But JE am just a rock" she replied.

"You are no longer just a rock like the day you left me," said the big blue planet. "You have GRANDIS bold and bright. Now you are a shooting star, and you are the RAISON that I shine. And while you are worrying about which direction to go, all of the planets in space are hoping that you will come their way to brighten them."

POURQUOI = Why	VU = Seen
MOI = Me	JE = I
GRANDIS = Grown	RAISON = Reason

And so the shooting star, QUI was no longer just a rock, finally understood. It did not matter OÙ she went, the light was her own.

So the rock sat there for a moment, by the bright blue planet and wondered.

 "Should I keep traveling, or should I fly AUTOUR the big blue planet and grow brighter with it each day."

She thought, until she knew exactly what to do.

QUI = Who
OÙ = Where
AUTOUR = Around

Story 2: THE ISLAND OF BUM BUM BA LOO

Have you sailed to the ÎLE of Bum Bum Ba Loo?
It's something that all GÉNIAL explorers must do

DIX years ago, I set off with my crew
In search of the island of Bum Bum Ba Loo

The VAGUE on the sea made me wish that I flew
To get to that island of Bum Bum Ba Loo

The path on my map led us slightly askew
And we sailed every ocean, before NOUS were
through

But when we arrived it was then that I knew
That all of the stories I heard must be VRAI

ÎLE = Island	GÉNIAL = Great
DIX = Ten	VAGUE = Waves
NOUS = We	VRAI = True

The EAU surrounding it shone a bright hue
A magnificent color, like no AUTRE blue

A sign made with vines, held together by glue,
Stood on the RIVAGE, reading "We Welcome You!"

The ROI had arranged for a great big to-do
And the queen herself shouted the loudest
"Woohoo!"

The Bum Bum Ba Lites gave us bowls of their stew
Which they made from the RACINE of the Great Bum
Ba Doo
The food could have fed SEPT hundred and two
At the feast on the Island of Bum Bum Ba Loo

EAU = Water   AUTRE = Other
RIVAGE = Shore   RACINE = Roots
SEPT = Seven

Our BOISSONS were quite tasty, a tropical brew
If you ask what was in them, I haven't a clue

They served us deserts made with Bum Berry goo
As we danced to the tune of the didgeridoo

We all thanked the King for the PARTIE he threw
Of course not forgetting to thank the Queen too

From their palace they showed us the wonderful
VUE
And we saw all the fields where the Bum Berries
grew

As CADEAU, I gave both of them gumballs to chew
When they asked me for more I had only few

BOISSONS = Drinks   PARTIE = Party
VUE = View   CADEAU = Gift

So we hopped on the BATEAU where we kept a
whole slew
But it got carried off when the northern VENT blew

The island has waited to be found anew
While I searched for someone to give the CARTE to

And now I've decided to DONNER it to you
To discover the island of Bum Bum Ba Loo

BATEAU = Ship   VENT = Wind
CARTE = Map   DONNER = Pass

Story 3: The Boy Who Cried Wolf

Once upon a time, there lived a BERGER boy who was bored watching his flock of MOUTON on the hill.
To amuse himself, he shouted, "Wolf! Wolf! The sheep are being chased by the wolf!" The villagers came running to help the boy and SAUVER the sheep. They found nothing and the boy just laughed looking at their angry faces.
"Don't cry 'wolf' when there's no wolf boy!", they said angrily and left. The boy just laughed at them.
After a while, he got bored and cried 'wolf!' again, fooling the villagers a second time. The angry VILLAGEOIS warned the boy a second time and left.

BERGER = Shepard   MOUTON = Sheep
SAUVER = Save   VILLAGEOIS = Villagers

The boy continued watching the TROUPEAU. After a while, he saw a real LOUP and cried loudly, "Wolf! Please help! The wolf is chasing the sheep. Help!" But this time, no one turned up to help. By evening, when the boy didn't return MAISON, the villagers wondered what happened to him and went up the hill. The boy sat on the hill weeping. "Why didn't you come when I called out that there was a wolf?" he asked angrily. "The flock is scattered now", he said. An old villager approached him and said, "People won't believe MENTEUR even when they tell the truth. We'll look for your sheep DEMAIN morning. Let's go home now".

TROUPEAU = Flock   LOUP = Wolf
MAISON = Home   MENTEURS = Liars
DEMAIN = Tomorrow

Once upon a time, a FERMIER had a goose that laid a golden egg every day. The OEUF provided enough ARGENT for the farmer and his wife for their day-to-day needs. The farmer and his FEMME were HEUREUX for a long time. But one day, the farmer got an idea and thought, "Why should I take just one egg a day? Why can't I take all of them at once and make a lot of money?"
The foolish farmer's wife also agreed and decided to cut the goose's stomach for the eggs. As soon as they TUER the bird and opened the goose's stomach, to find nothing but guts and blood. The farmer, realizing his foolish ERREUR, cries over the lost resource!

FERMIER = Farmer   ŒUF = Egg
ARGENT = Money   FEMME = Wife
HEUREUX = Happy   TUER = Killed
ERREUR = Mistake

Story 5: *The Ant And The Grasshopper*

One bright day in late AUTOMNE a family of FOURMI
were bustling about in the warm sunshine, drying
out the GRAINE they had stored up during the
summer, when a starving Grasshopper, his fiddle
under his arm, came up and humbly begged for a
bite to MANGER.
"What!" cried the Ants in surprise, "haven't you
stored anything away for the winter? What in the
world were you doing all last summer?"
"I didn't have time to store up any NOURITURE,"
whined the Grasshopper; "I was so OCCUPÉ
making music that before I knew it the summer
was PARTI."
The Ants shrugged their shoulders in disgust.
"Making music, were you?" they cried. "Very well;
now dance!" And they turned their backs on the
Grasshopper and went on with their work.
There's a time for work and a time for play.

AUTOMNE = Automn   FOURMI = Ants
GRAINE = Grain   MANGER = Eat
NOURRITURE = Food   OCCUPÉ = Busy
PARTI = Gone

Story 6: *The Lion and the Mouse*

A lion was once DORMIR in the jungle when a SOURIS started running up and down his body just for fun. This disturbed the lion's sleep, and he woke up quite FÂCHÉ. He was about to eat the mouse when the mouse desperately requested the lion to set him free. "I promise you, I will be of great help to you someday if you save me." The lion laughed at the mouse's confidence and let him go.
One day, a few CHASEURS came into the forest and took the lion with them. They tied him up against a tree. The lion was struggling to get out and started to whimper. Soon, the mouse walked past and noticed the lion in trouble. RAPIDEMENT, he ran and gnawed on the ropes to set the lion LIBRE. Both of them sped off into the jungle.
A small act of kindness can go a long way.

DORMIR = Sleeping
FÂCHÉ = Angry
RAPIDEMENT = Quickly

SOURIS = Mouse
CHASEURS = Hunters
LIBRE = Free

Story 7: *When Adversity Knocks*

There was a FILLE named Asha who lived with her mother and father in a village. One day, her father assigned her a simple task. He took TROIS vessels filled with boiling water. He placed an egg in one vessel, a potato in the second vessel, and some tea leaves in the third vessel. He asked Asha to keep an eye on the vessels POUR about ten to fifteen minutes while the three ingredients in three separate vessels boiled. After the said time, he asked Asha to peel the PATATE and egg, and strain the tea leaves. Asha was left puzzled she understood her father was trying to EXPLIQUER her something, but she didn't know what it was.
Her father explained, "All three items were put in the same circumstances. See how they've responded DIFFÉREMMENT." He said that the potato turned soft, the egg turned hard, and the tea leaves changed the COULEUR and taste of the water. "We are all like one of these items. When adversity calls, we respond exactly the way they do. Now, are you a potato, an egg, or tea leaves?"
We can choose how to respond to a difficult situation.

FILLE = Girl   TROIS = Three
POUR = For   PATATE = Potato
EXPLIQUER = Explain   DIFFÉREMMENT = Differently
COULEUR = Color

Story 8: The Cows And The Tiger

Four cows lived in a FORÊT near a meadow. They were good AMIS and did everything together. They grazed together and stayed together, because of which no tigers or lions were able to kill them for food.
But one day, the friends fought and each cow went to graze in a different direction. A tiger and a lion saw this and decided that it was the perfect opportunity to kill the VACHES. They hid in the bushes and surprised the cows and killed them all, one by one.
Unity is strength.

FORÊT = Forest　　　　AMIS = Friends
VACHE = Cows

Story 9: The Camel And The Baby

One day, a camel and her BÉBÉ were chatting. The baby asked, "MAMAN, why do we have humps?" The mother replied, "Our humps are for storing water so that we can survive in the desert".

"Oh", said the child, "and why do we have rounded feet mother?" "Because they are meant to AIDER us walk comfortably in the desert. These legs help us move around in the sand."

"Alright. But why are our eyelashes so long?" "To protect our YEUX from the desert dust and sand. They are the protective covers for the eyes", replied the mother camel.

The baby camel thought for a while and said, "So we have humps to store water for desert journeys, rounded hooves to keep us comfortable when we MARCHER in the desert sand, and long eyelashes to protect us from sand and dust during a desert storm. Then what are we doing in a zoo?"

The mother was dumbfounded.

Your strengths, skills, and knowledge are useless if you are not in the right place.

BÉBÉ = Baby   MAMAN = Mother
AIDER = Help   YEUX = Eyes
MARCHER = Walk

Story 10: The Wolf And The Shepherds

One day a wolf was chased away from a farm for ESSAYER to steal some of the sheep for food. Later that SEMAINE, the wolf came back to the farm hoping to find some food. He peeped inside the MAISON and found the farmer and his family feasting on lamb roast.

"Aha!", he thought. "If I were to do the same CHOSE that the farmer and his family are doing now, I would be shunted and chased, or even killed for killing a FAIBLE, innocent lamb."

We are quick to judge and condemn others for what they do, but see nothing wrong in doing so ourselves.

ESSAYER = Trying   SEMAINE = Week
MAISON = House   CHOSE = Thing
FAIBLE = Weak

Story 11: The Fox and the Stork

One day, a selfish RENARD invited a stork for dinner. Stork was very CONTENT with the invitation she reached the fox's home on time and knocked at the PORTE with her long beak. The fox took her to the dinner table and served some soup in shallow bowls for both of them. As the bowl was too shallow for the stork, she couldn't have soup at all. But, the fox licked up his soup quickly.
The stork was angry and upset, but she didn't show her anger and behaved politely. To APPRENDRE a lesson to the fox, she then invited him for dinner the next day. She too served soup, but this time the soup was served in two LONG narrow vases. The stork devoured the soup from her vase, but the fox couldn't drink any of it because of his narrow neck. The fox realised his mistake and went home famished.
A selfish act backfires sooner or later!

RENARD = Fox   CONTENT = Happy
PORTE = Door   APPRENDRE = Learn
LONG = Tall

Story 12: The Dog At The Well

A dog and her pups lived on a farm, where there was a PUIT. The mother dog told the pups, do not go near the well or JOUER around it. One of the pups wondered why they shouldn't go to the well and decided to explore it. He went to the well. Climbed up the wall and peeked inside.
In there, he saw his reflection and thought it was AUTRE dog. The pup saw that the other CHIEN in the well (his reflection) was doing whatever he was doing, and got angry for imitating him. He decided to fight with the dog and jumped into the well, only to find no dog there. He barked and barked and swam until the farmer came and rescued him. The pup had learned his lesson. *Always listen to what the elders say. Question them, but do not defy them.*

PUIT = **Well**   JOUER = **Play**
AUTRE = **Other**   CHIEN = **Dog**

Story 13: The Crystal Ball

Nasir, a small GARÇON, found a crystal ball behind the banyan ARBRE of his garden. The ARBRE told him that it would grant him a wish. He was very happy and he thought hard, but unfortunately, he could not come up with anything he wanted. So, he kept the crystal ball in his bag and waited until he could decide on his wish.

Days went by without him making a wish but his MEILLEUR friend saw him looking at the crystal ball. He stole it from Nasir and showed it to everyone in the village. They all asked for palaces and riches and BEAUCOUP of gold, but could not make more than one wish. In the end, everyone was angry because no one could have everything they wanted. They became very unhappy and decided to ask Nasir for AIDE.

Nasir wished that everything would go back to how it was once? before the villagers had tried to satisfy their greed. The palaces and OR vanished and the villagers once again became happy and content.

GARÇON = Boy	ARBRE = Tree
MEILLEUR = Best	BEAUCOUP = Lots
AIDE = Help	OR = Gold

Story 14: The Crystal Ball

Once upon a time, three VOISINS living in a village were having trouble with LEURS crops. Each of the neighbours had one field, but the crops on their fields were infested with pests and were wilting. CHAQUE day, they would come up with different ideas to help their crops. The first one tried using a scarecrow in his CHAMP, the second used pesticides, and the third built a fence on his field, all to no avail.
One day, the village head came by and APPELER the three farmers. He gave them each a stick and asked them to break it. The farmers could CASSER them easily. He then gave them a bundle of three sticks, and again, asked them to break it. This time, the farmers struggled to break the BATONS. The village head said, "Together, you are stronger and work better than you do it alone." The farmers understood what the village head was saying. They pooled in their resources and got rid of the pests from their fields.
There is strength in unity.

VOISINS = Neighbours   LEURS = Their
CHAQUE = Every   CHAMP = Field
APPELER = Called   CASSER = Break
BATONS = Stick

Story 15: The Man And The Cat

One day, a HOMME was walking by a road when he heard a CHAT meowing from the bushes nearby.
The cat was stuck and needed help getting out.
When the man reached out, the cat got scared and scratched the man. The man screamed in pain but didn't back down. He tried again and again, even as the cat continued to scratch his hands.
Another passerby saw this and said, "Just let it be! The cat will find a way to come out later". The man didn't pay heed but tried JUSQU'A he helped the cat. Once he let the cat LIBRE, he told the other man, "The cat is an animal, and its instincts make him scratch and attack. I am a human and my instincts make me compassionate and GENTIL".
Treat everyone around you like you want to be treated. Adhere to your own rules or ethics, not theirs.

HOMME = Man   CHAT = Cat
JUSQU'À = Until   LIBRE = Free
GENTIL = Kind